This book was compiled by Daniel Melehi
with the A.I assistance of Inventabot

Dedication

I hope this helps all of my wonderful
readers achieve all their goals in their
business. And I would like to thank my
wonderful wife for all of her continued
support in all my ventures.

May 7 2023

Contents

Chapter 1: Introduction to Joomla Plugins 8

Subchapter 1.1: What are Joomla Plugins? 8

Subchapter 1.2: Why Create Custom Joomla Plugins? 9

Subchapter 1.1: What are Joomla Plugins? 9

Why Create Custom Joomla Plugins? 10

Chapter 2: Understanding Plugin Structures 12

Subchapter 2.1: Joomla Plugin File Structure 12

Subchapter 2.2: Plugin Events and Triggers 13

Subchapter 2.3: Plugin Parameters and Settings............13

Understanding Joomla Plugin File Structure 14

Plugin Events and Triggers...15

Plugin Parameters and Settings....................................17

Chapter 3: Creating Your First Custom Joomla Plugin...19

Subchapter 3.1: Setting up Your Development
Environment 20

Subchapter 3.2: Creating a Simple Plugin 20

    myplugin.php 21

    myplugin.xml 21

Subchapter 3.3: Testing and Debugging Your Plugin 22

Setting up Your Development Environment 23

Creating a Simple Plugin...25

Subchapter 3.3: Testing and Debugging Your Plugin 27

Chapter 4: Advanced Plugin Development Techniques .29

Subchapter 4.1: Plugin Security Best Practices...............29

Subchapter 4.2: Database Integration with Plugins 30

Subchapter 4.3: Creating Multi-language Plugins...........31

Plugin Security Best Practices 32
Sanitize and Validate User Input 32
Use Joomla APIs 33
Use Strong Encryption Algorithms 33
Follow Least Privilege 33
Keep Your Plugins Updated 34

Subchapter 4.2: Database Integration with Plugins 34

Creating Multi-language Plugins.....................................36

Chapter 5: Packaging and Distributing Your Plugin 38

Subchapter 5.1: Creating the Plugin Installation Package38

Subchapter 5.2: Distributing Your Plugin through the
Joomla Extension Directory 40

Subchapter 5.3: Marketing and Promoting Your Plugin ..41
Conclusion: 41

Creating the Plugin Installation Package........................42

Distributing Your Plugin through the Joomla Extension
Directory 44

Marketing and Promoting Your Plugin...........................46
1. Submitting Your Plugin to the Joomla Extension Directory
....46

2. Creating a Website and Social Media Pages for Your Plugin 47

3. Partnering with Other Developers and Websites.............47

4. Offering Discounts and Incentives.................................48

5. Providing Excellent Support and Customer Service 48

Chapter 6: Best Practices and Tips for Plugin Development 49

Subchapter 6.1: Code Standards and Guidelines.............49

1. Use Proper Indentation 50

2. Follow Naming Conventions.............................50

3. Use Proper Commenting 50

Subchapter 6.2: Choosing the Right Plugin Type 51

1. Content Plugins 51

2. System Plugins...51

3. User Plugins...52

Subchapter 6.3: Tips for Efficient Plugin Development ...52

1. Avoid Duplicate Code 52

2. Test Your Plugins 53

3. Keep Your Code Modular 53

Code Standards and Guidelines 53

Subchapter 6.3: Tips for Efficient Plugin Development ...57

1. Plan Ahead...57

2. Use Reusable Code 57

3. Optimize Your Code......................................58

4. Keep Up-to-Date with Joomla 58

5. Use a Testing Methodology.............................58

Chapter 7: Troubleshooting and Common Errors..........59

Subchapter 7.1: Debugging Tips for Plugin Developers ...60

Subchapter 7.2: Common Plugin Development Errors and How to Fix Them **61**

Common Plugin Development Errors and How to Fix Them **64**

    1. Syntax Errors 64

    2. Undefined Variables 65

    3. Function Name Errors 65

    4. White Screen of Death 66

    5. Database Errors 66

Chapter 1: Introduction to Joomla Plugins Joomla is a popular and powerful content management system that allows developers to create customizable websites and applications. One of the key features of Joomla is its plugin architecture, which allows for the creation of custom extensions that can enhance the functionality of a Joomla site. In this book, we will explore the world of Joomla plugins and teach you everything you need to know to create your own custom plugins. Whether you are a seasoned developer or just starting out, this book will provide you with the knowledge and skills necessary to build powerful and flexible plugins that take your Joomla site to the next level. We will begin by discussing what Joomla plugins are and why you might want to create your own. We will then dive into the structure of Joomla plugins, including their file structure, events, and triggers, as well as parameters and settings.

From there, we will guide you through the process of creating your first custom Joomla plugin, including setting up your development environment, creating a simple plugin, and testing and debugging your code. Next, we will cover more advanced techniques for plugin development, such as security best practices, database integration, and creating multi-language plugins. We will also discuss how to package and distribute your plugin, including creating installation packages and promoting your plugin through the Joomla Extension Directory. Finally, we will provide some best practices and tips for plugin development, as well as troubleshooting common errors and debugging your code. By the end of this book, you will have the knowledge and skills necessary to create your own custom Joomla plugins, and take your Joomla site to the next level of functionality and customization. So let's get started!

Chapter 1: Introduction to Joomla Plugins

Joomla is a powerful and popular CMS platform that enables users to create powerful, dynamic websites with ease. One of the most exciting features of Joomla is its expansive plugin architecture that allows users to extend the core system with custom functionality.

SUBCHAPTER 1.1: WHAT ARE JOOMLA PLUGINS?

Joomla plugins are a type of extension that can modify the behavior of a Joomla website. A plugin allows developers to add custom functionality, modify existing functionality, or create new triggers that can be used to execute custom code.

SUBCHAPTER 1.2: WHY CREATE CUSTOM JOOMLA PLUGINS?

Creating custom Joomla plugins offers several advantages for developers and website owners. By developing custom plugins, developers can enhance website functionality to meet specific requirements and create a more personalized website experience. Additionally, plugins can be shared with the broader Joomla community, leading to greater recognition and reputation. In the next chapter, we will discuss the structure of Joomla plugins and the various events and triggers that can be used to execute custom code.

SUBCHAPTER 1.1: WHAT ARE JOOMLA PLUGINS?

Joomla plugins are powerful tools that allow you to extend the functionality of your Joomla website beyond what is built-in by default. They can add extra features, customize the behavior of core functions, and introduce new capabilities altogether. Simply put, Joomla plugins are code snippets that are triggered by specific events or conditions, allowing you to write custom code that changes how Joomla behaves. For example, you could create a plugin that automatically generates a sitemap for your website or one that removes certain sections of content from appearing on certain pages. These types of customization are what make Joomla plugins so versatile and valuable. There are many different types of Joomla plugins, including content, system, user, and search plugins. Each type has a specific purpose and set of events that it can listen for. Throughout this book, we'll explore these different types of plugins in more detail.

WHY CREATE CUSTOM JOOMLA PLUGINS?

Joomla comes with a wide range of core functionality which caters to the needs of most users, but sometimes you may require additional functionality or customization that is not available out of the box. Creating custom plugins is the solution to such scenarios. Plugins give you the flexibility to extend Joomla's functionality and customize how it behaves. They allow you to add new features, manipulate existing ones, and tweak the behavior of your Joomla site according to your specific needs. Creating custom Joomla plugins has a number of benefits. It allows you to: - Enhance site functionality: Custom plugins enable you to extend the existing functionality of your Joomla site with your own unique features and functionality. - Tailor your site: Every Joomla site is unique, so custom plugins allow you to tailor your site to your specific needs. This can include everything from custom layouts to specific functionality that you require. - Increase efficiency: Custom plugins can help save you time and increase the efficiency of your site. By automating tasks or streamlining processes, you can focus on what matters most - the content and growth of your website. - Improve SEO: By developing custom plugins, you have the ability to improve your site's search engine optimization. You can add custom meta tags, improve site speed, and more. Overall, custom plugins can help you achieve your goals and take your Joomla site to the next level. In the next chapter, we'll dive deeper into the structure of Joomla plugins to better understand how they work.

Chapter 2: Understanding Plugin Structures

Joomla plugins are essential components that allow developers to extend and modify the core functionality of Joomla. In this chapter, we will take a closer look at the different structures and elements that make up Joomla plugins.

SUBCHAPTER 2.1: JOOMLA PLUGIN FILE STRUCTURE

Joomla plugins are usually packaged as a single .zip file that contains all the necessary files and folders to make the plugin work. A typical plugin will include a folder with the plugin name that contains the plugin's main PHP file, a language folder for language files, and a metadata.xml file that holds information about the plugin.

SUBCHAPTER 2.2: PLUGIN EVENTS AND TRIGGERS

Plugins are triggered or called by specific events that occur within the Joomla system. These events are defined in the core Joomla code and can be extended by developers to include custom events. Some common plugin events include onContentBeforeSave, onUserLogin, and onAfterRender.

SUBCHAPTER 2.3: PLUGIN PARAMETERS AND SETTINGS

Plugins can also have parameters and settings that can be configured by users. These settings can control the behavior and output of the plugin, and can be accessed and modified through the Joomla administrator interface. Understanding the different elements and structures of Joomla plugins is crucial for any developer looking to create custom plugins for Joomla. In the next chapter, we will take a closer look at the process of creating your first custom Joomla plugin.

UNDERSTANDING JOOMLA PLUGIN FILE STRUCTURE

As a Joomla developer, understanding the file structure of a plugin is essential. A typical Joomla plugin consists of a single PHP file and an optional XML file that provides metadata about the plugin. The PHP file is the core of the plugin and has a specific naming convention that indicates the type of plugin it is. For example, a content plugin will have a name starting with "plg_content_", while a system plugin will have a name starting with "plg_system_". The PHP file contains the code that will be executed when the plugin is triggered by an event or hook in Joomla. This code should be well-structured and properly commented for clarity and future maintainability. In addition, the optional XML file provides additional information about the plugin, such as its name, version, author, and description. It is also used to specify any plugin options or parameters that can be configured in the Joomla backend. Understanding the file structure of a Joomla plugin is crucial for developing custom plugins that integrate seamlessly with Joomla's architecture. In the next subchapter, we will explore Joomla's plugin event system, which is what allows plugins to interact with Joomla's core functionality.

PLUGIN EVENTS AND TRIGGERS

Joomla plugins allow developers to respond to specific events or triggers within the Joomla system. An event can be thought of as an action that occurs within the Joomla framework, such as a user logging in or content being saved. A trigger, on the other hand, is code that executes when a specific event occurs. Plugins are triggered by hooks within the Joomla core. Joomla has many different events that can be acted upon using plugins, including user authentication, content editing, and component initialization. When a plugin is triggered, its code is executed and it has the ability to modify or extend the behavior of the Joomla system. Developers can create their own custom events and triggers within their plugins to respond to specific actions or behaviors within their custom components or modules. These custom events and triggers allow for greater flexibility and customization within Joomla-based websites. Understanding events and triggers is essential for creating effective Joomla plugins. As a developer, it is important to identify the specific event or trigger that you want to respond to, and then write code that executes when that occurs. With careful attention to triggers and events, you can create highly customized and powerful Joomla plugins.

PLUGIN PARAMETERS AND SETTINGS

Plugin parameters and settings are an essential part of developing custom Joomla plugins. These parameters allow users to customize the plugin's behavior to suit their specific needs without requiring any modification to the plugin's code. **What are Plugin Parameters?** Plugin parameters are variables that can be configured by the user to modify the behavior of a plugin. These parameters can be defined in the plugin's XML file and accessed within the plugin code using the JFactory class. For example, a plugin that displays a message to the user could have a parameter for the message's text. By providing a default value for this parameter in the plugin's XML file, the plugin will display the default message when installed but allow users to customize the message if they want to. **Defining Plugin Parameters** To define a plugin parameter, you must include a `params` section in the plugin's XML file. This section should contain one or more `param` elements, each of which defines a single parameter. A `param` element can have several attributes, including: - `name`: The name of the parameter - `type`: The data type of the parameter (e.g. text, integer, boolean, etc.) -

`default:` The default value of the parameter - `label:` The label for the parameter to be displayed in the plugin configuration settings For example: `<params>` `<param name="message" type="text" default="Hello World!" label="Message Text" />` `</params>` This would define a parameter named 'message' with a data type of text, a default value of 'Hello World!', and a label of 'Message Text'. **Accessing Plugin Parameters in Code** Once you've defined plugin parameters in the XML file, you can access them in the plugin's PHP code using the JFactory class. The following code demonstrates how to get the value of a parameter named 'message': `$params = JFactory::getApplication()->getParams(); $message = $params->get('message', 'Default Message');` In this example, we first retrieve the plugin's parameters using the JFactory class. We then use the `get()` method to retrieve the value of the 'message' parameter. The second argument to `get()` specifies the default value to use if the parameter has not been set by the user. **Conclusion** By utilizing plugin parameters, you can make your custom Joomla plugins more flexible and user-friendly. With just a little bit of extra effort, you can allow users to customize your plugin's behavior without requiring them to modify any code.

Chapter 3: Creating Your First Custom Joomla Plugin

Now that we have a better understanding of Joomla plugins and their structures, let us dive into creating our own custom Joomla plugins. In this chapter, we will guide you through the process of creating your first custom Joomla plugin.

SUBCHAPTER 3.1: SETTING UP YOUR DEVELOPMENT ENVIRONMENT

Before diving into creating your first Joomla plugin, let us first set up our development environment. To develop

Joomla plugins locally, you will need to install a local development server like XAMPP or WAMP. These servers will allow you to run Joomla on your local machine, enabling you to develop and test your plugins without affecting the live site. After installing a local development server, the next step is to install the Joomla CMS. You can download Joomla's latest version from their official website and follow the installation process.

SUBCHAPTER 3.2: CREATING A SIMPLE PLUGIN

To create a Joomla plugin, you will need to create a new directory in the 'plugins' folder of your Joomla site. The directory name should match the name of your plugin, and the files should follow Joomla's plugin structure. A simple plugin can be created by creating two files, 'myplugin.php' and 'myplugin.xml'. The PHP file contains the plugin code, while the XML file defines the plugin metadata, including the plugin name, description, type, and other attributes. Here is an example of a simple 'Hello World' plugin: [CODE]

myplugin.php

defined('_JEXEC') or die; class plgContentMyplugin extends JPlugin { public function onContentPrepare($context, &$article, &$params, $page = 0) { $article->title = "Hello, World!"; $article->text .= " This is my first Joomla plugin!"; } }

myplugin.xml

Content - My Plugin 1.0 My first content plugin! myplugin.php [/CODE] Once you have created your plugin files, install the plugin through the Joomla administrator panel. After installation, enable the plugin, and you should see the "Hello, World!" message in your Joomla articles.

SUBCHAPTER 3.3: TESTING AND DEBUGGING YOUR PLUGIN

Testing and debugging your Joomla plugin is an essential part of the plugin development process. Joomla provides a built-in debugging tool that can help you test and debug your plugins. To enable Joomla's debugging tool, navigate to the Joomla global configuration page and click on the 'System' tab. In the 'Debug Settings' section, set the 'Debug System' and 'Debug Language' options to 'Yes'. With the debugging tool enabled, you can now view the debugging messages in your browser console, helping you to find and fix any errors in your custom Joomla plugin. In the next chapter, we will cover more advanced plugin development techniques, including plugin security best practices, database integration with plugins, and creating multi-language plugins.

SETTING UP YOUR DEVELOPMENT ENVIRONMENT

Before you start creating your custom Joomla plugin, you need to ensure that you have a proper development environment set up. This will help you in testing and debugging your plugin without affecting your production site. The first thing you need to do is to set up a local development environment. This can be done using software like XAMPP or WAMP. You can choose the software that suits your needs the best. Once you have installed the software, make sure that it is up and running by launching the control panel. After that, you will need to install Joomla on your local development environment by downloading the latest version from the official website. Make sure that you follow the installation instructions carefully to avoid any issues. Once Joomla is installed, you can start creating your custom plugin. It is recommended that you use a code editor like Visual Studio Code or Sublime Text to write your plugin code. This will make it easier for you to debug and test your plugin. It is also important to have a good understanding of PHP, HTML, CSS, and JavaScript when creating a custom Joomla plugin. If you are not proficient in these languages, it is recommended that you take some online courses or tutorials to gain the necessary skills. Finally, it is important that you have a version control system like Git set up. This will help you to keep track of changes to your plugin code and manage different versions of your plugin. In summary, before you start creating your custom Joomla plugin, you need to set up a local development environment, install Joomla, choose a code editor, have a good understanding of programming languages, and set up a version control system.

CREATING A SIMPLE PLUGIN

Now that you have set up your development environment, it's time to dive into creating your custom Joomla plugin. In this subchapter, we will focus on creating a simple plugin to get you started. The first step is to decide which type of plugin you want to create. Let's say you want to create a content plugin that adds a custom message to the end of every article on your Joomla site. To do this, you need to create a new PHP file in your plugin folder with a unique name that describes the plugin's purpose. For instance, you can name the file "mycustommessage.php". Once you have created the file, you need to add the plugin code. The Joomla plugin consists of a class definition, which includes the name of the plugin, the type of plugin, and the various functions that will be called by Joomla. Here's an example of the code you can use to create your custom message plugin: ```
text is also available * @param object

&$params The articles params * @param integer $page The 'page' number * * @return boolean True on success */ public function onContentPrepare($context, &$article, &$params, $page = 0) { // Check to make sure we're in the right context if ($context != 'com_content.article') { return true; } // Add custom message to the end of article text $article->text .= '

Thank you for reading our article. If you have any questions, please contact us.

'; return true; } } ?> ``` The code above creates a new class named "plgContentMycustommessage" that extends the JPlugin class. It includes two functions: a constructor that calls the parent constructor and the "onContentPrepare" function. The "onContentPrepare" function is the one that modifies the article text by adding a custom message at the end of the text. Once you have created the PHP file and added the plugin code, you need to install and enable the plugin through the Joomla administration panel. Once the plugin is enabled, every article on your site will display the custom message you added. In the next subchapter, we will cover how to test and debug your plugin code to ensure it is working correctly.

SUBCHAPTER 3.3: TESTING AND DEBUGGING YOUR PLUGIN

Testing and debugging are crucial steps in developing a custom Joomla plugin. You want to make sure that your plugin performs as expected with no errors or issues. To test your plugin, you can use Joomla's built-in plugin manager. First, install your plugin package just as you would any other extension in Joomla. Then, navigate to the Plugin Manager in the backend of your website. You should see your newly installed plugin listed there. To test your plugin, enable it by clicking on the green checkmark icon next to its name. Then, navigate to the frontend of your website and test the functionality of your plugin. Keep an eye out for any errors or unexpected behaviors. To debug your plugin, you can use Joomla's built-in debugging tools. First, make sure that Joomla's debugging mode is enabled in your website's global configuration. Then, navigate to your plugin's code and add some debug statements using Joomla's JLog function. These statements will output to Joomla's debug log file, which you can access through Joomla's backend. Once you have identified any issues with your plugin, use the debugging information to fix any errors or unexpected behaviors. Debugging can be a time-consuming process, but it is worth it to ensure that your plugin works as intended. Remember to always test and debug your plugin thoroughly before distributing it to others. A well-tested and debugged plugin will help your users avoid frustration and ensure that your plugin is well-received in the Joomla community.

Chapter 4: Advanced Plugin Development Techniques

SUBCHAPTER 4.1: PLUGIN SECURITY BEST PRACTICES

When developing custom Joomla plugins, it's important to consider security as a top priority. One of the first things you should always do is sanitize any user input to prevent attacks such as SQL injection or cross-site scripting (XSS). Another best practice is to avoid using hardcoded credentials or sensitive information in your code. It's recommended to store sensitive information such as API keys or database credentials in a configuration file, which can be excluded from version control to prevent accidental exposure. You should also validate any data coming from external sources or user input. Don't blindly trust any data that's not coming from your own code, as it may include malicious content. Finally, be sure to keep your plugins up-to-date and monitor for any security vulnerabilities that may arise in the future. Always follow industry-standard security practices and guidelines to protect your users and their data.

SUBCHAPTER 4.2: DATABASE INTEGRATION WITH PLUGINS

Plugins often need to interact with databases to store or retrieve data. When developing custom Joomla plugins, it's important to know how to properly integrate with the Joomla database. Joomla provides a database abstraction layer that allows you to perform CRUD (Create, Read, Update, Delete) operations on the database. You should always use this layer to ensure compatibility with different databases and prevent potential security vulnerabilities. When writing SQL queries, it's important to follow best practices such as parameterized queries and avoiding hardcoded values.

This will minimize the risk of SQL injection attacks. Additionally, you should be aware of Joomla's database prefixing feature, which allows for different database table prefix values based on the Joomla installation. Always use the appropriate prefix when interacting with the database to ensure compatibility and prevent conflicts.

SUBCHAPTER 4.3: CREATING MULTI-LANGUAGE PLUGINS

One of the key features of Joomla is its multi-language support. This means that plugins should also provide support for multiple languages to ensure a seamless user experience for all users. To create a multi-language plugin, you should start by defining the set of strings that need to be translated. Use the Joomla language files to define these strings and their translations for each supported language. Once you have defined the language strings, you can use Joomla's language functions to display the appropriate strings based on the active language. This will ensure that users see the plugin content in their preferred language. You should also ensure that any user input, such as form fields or URLs, is properly translated and respects the active language. Always test your plugin thoroughly to ensure that all strings are being translated correctly and that the user experience is seamless in all supported languages.

PLUGIN SECURITY BEST PRACTICES

When developing custom plugins for Joomla, security should always be a top priority. Here are some best practices to keep in mind:

Sanitize and Validate User Input

User input can provide an entry point for attackers to exploit and compromise your website. It is essential to sanitize and validate all user input data before using it within your Joomla plugin. This helps to prevent SQL injection, Cross-Site Scripting (XSS), and other similar attacks.

Use Joomla APIs

Joomla provides a wide range of APIs to developers. These APIs have been developed to work within the Joomla framework, so it is recommended to use them instead of custom coding. Using these APIs ensures that your plugin interacts with the Joomla system in a secure and standardized way.

Use Strong Encryption Algorithms

If your plugin handles sensitive data, it is essential to encrypt it using strong encryption algorithms like AES or RSA. The use of weak encryption algorithms can lead to data breaches, which can be detrimental to the reputation of your website.

Follow Least Privilege

When coding a plugin, it is best to follow the principle of least privilege. This means giving applications and users only the minimum permissions necessary to perform their functions. This can help to mitigate the impact of a security breach by limiting the access of compromised accounts.

Keep Your Plugins Updated

Keeping your plugins updated is crucial to maintaining the security of your website. Regular updates ensure that your plugin is protected from known vulnerabilities and exploits. It is recommended to stay current with the latest Joomla releases and to update your plugin accordingly. By following these best practices, you can ensure that your Joomla plugin is secure and protected from attackers looking to exploit vulnerabilities.

SUBCHAPTER 4.2: DATABASE INTEGRATION WITH PLUGINS

Plugins play a crucial role in Joomla's database integration. Custom plugins can be developed to interact with Joomla's database and perform operations such as inserting data, updating data, deleting data, and retrieving data from the database. One of the most important things to consider when creating a plugin is security. It is important to secure the data that is being transferred between the plugin and the database. Joomla provides robust classes for handling database interactions, including classes for SQL statements and database queries. One important decision when developing a plugin that integrates with the database is choosing which Joomla database layer to use. Joomla provides two database layers: JDatabase and JDatabaseDriver. JDatabase is the original database layer for Joomla, while JDatabaseDriver is the newer, more flexible, and faster database layer. When choosing which database layer to use, it is important to consider the specific needs of your plugin. If your plugin needs to interact with a specific database, you may want to use the JDatabase layer. If your plugin needs to support multiple databases, you may want to use the JDatabaseDriver layer. Another consideration when developing a plugin that interacts with the database is which database engine to use. Joomla supports a variety of database engines, including MySQL, PostgreSQL, and SQLite. Each database engine has its own strengths and weaknesses, so it is important to choose the one that is most appropriate for your plugin's needs. In addition to the database engine, it is important to consider the structure of the database itself. Your plugin should be designed to work with the structure of the database, including tables, columns, and relationships. It is also important to consider table prefixes, which are used to help prevent naming conflicts between Joomla and other extensions.

Overall, database integration is an important consideration when developing a custom plugin for Joomla. By carefully considering the security, database layer, database engine, and database structure, you can create a custom plugin that integrates seamlessly with Joomla's database.

CREATING MULTI-LANGUAGE PLUGINS

In today's globalized world, it's essential for websites to be available in multiple languages. Joomla has made it easy to achieve this through its Multi-language capabilities. By creating multi-language plugins, you can save the hassle of manually translating multiple language versions of your plugin. To create a multi-language plugin, you must first identify the text that needs to be translated. This text can either be static or dynamic. Static text is hardcoded into the plugin file, while dynamic text is content that is generated at runtime. To translate static text, you should add language strings to your plugin XML file and place it in the language folder of your plugin. Each language file must be named after the language code and saved in the appropriate folder. For dynamic content, the translation can be handled by Joomla's language filter. You should place all language-specific content in language string files and use the language filter to display the appropriate content based on the user's language preference. It's essential to keep in mind that not all languages are written the same way, and some languages use different character sets. Your plugin should be able to handle these differences gracefully. Joomla's UTF-8 encoding standard allows for seamless integration of different character sets. By following these guidelines, you can create a truly multi-language plugin that will be accessible to users all around the world.

Chapter 5: Packaging and Distributing Your Plugin

Packaging and distributing your plugin is an important step towards making it accessible to the wider Joomla community. Luckily, Joomla provides a simple and straightforward process for creating an installation package for your plugin.

SUBCHAPTER 5.1: CREATING THE PLUGIN INSTALLATION PACKAGE

To create an installation package for your plugin, you will need to create a zip file that contains all of the necessary files and directories for your plugin. This includes the plugin entry file, any additional files needed by the plugin, and any language files required. Once you have gathered all of the necessary files, you can create a zip file using your favorite compression tool, such as 7-Zip or WinZip. Make sure that the zip file is named using the following naming convention:

plg_{plugin_type}_{plugin_name}_{versio n}.zip. For example, if your plugin is named "myplugin" and is of the type "system", and the version is "1.0.0", the file name would be: plg_system_myplugin_1.0.0.zip. After creating the installation package, you can upload it to your Joomla site and install it like any other third-party extension. You can also distribute it through the Joomla Extension Directory (JED) to make it accessible to the wider Joomla community.

SUBCHAPTER 5.2: DISTRIBUTING YOUR PLUGIN THROUGH THE JOOMLA EXTENSION DIRECTORY

To distribute your plugin through the Joomla Extension Directory, you will need to create an account on the JED website and submit your plugin for approval. This process typically involves filling out a form with information about your plugin, uploading the installation package, and providing any additional details or documentation. After your plugin has been approved, it will be accessible to the wider Joomla community for download and installation. This can increase the visibility of your plugin and help you reach a larger audience.

SUBCHAPTER 5.3: MARKETING AND PROMOTING YOUR PLUGIN

In addition to packaging and distributing your plugin, it can also be helpful to promote it through other channels, such as social media, forums, and targeted advertising. By building a strong online presence and reaching out to potential users, you can help build awareness and generate interest in your plugin. Some tips for successfully marketing and promoting your plugin include creating a strong and memorable branding, creating engaging and informative demo videos or tutorials, and actively engaging with your audience through social media and other channels.

Conclusion:

Packaging and distributing your plugin is an important step towards making it accessible to the wider Joomla community. By following the simple process outlined in this chapter, you can create and distribute your plugin with ease and help it reach a larger audience. Additionally, marketing and promoting your plugin can help build awareness and generate interest, leading to increased adoption and success.

CREATING THE PLUGIN INSTALLATION PACKAGE

After you have created your custom Joomla plugin, you'll need to package it for distribution. Fortunately, Joomla makes this process easy with its built-in Extension Manager. Here's how to package your plugin for installation: 1. Create a new folder on your computer and give it a name that describes your plugin. 2. Inside this folder, create a folder named "plugin". This is where you'll put the files for your plugin. 3. Copy all of the files for your plugin into the "plugin" folder. Make sure you include any necessary language files, images, and other assets. 4. Create a new file in the main folder called "index.html" and put some basic information about your plugin in this file, such as the name, version, and a brief description. 5. Create a new file in the main folder called "manifest.xml". This file contains metadata about your plugin and tells Joomla how to install and uninstall it. Here's an example of what your manifest file might look like: ``` My Custom Plugin April 3, 2022 John Doe john.doe@example.com 1.0.0 A custom Joomla plugin for doing X and Y. my_custom_plugin.php ``` 6. Save your manifest file and make sure it's named "manifest.xml". 7. Zip up the main folder (not just the "plugin" folder). You should end up with a zip file containing the main folder, the "plugin" folder, and the two additional files you created. 8. Your installation package is now ready! You can test it out by installing it on a Joomla test site or submitting it to the Joomla Extension Directory for distribution. Congratulations! You now know how to create an installation package for your custom Joomla plugin. This step is crucial for making your plugin easy for others to install and use.

DISTRIBUTING YOUR PLUGIN THROUGH THE JOOMLA EXTENSION DIRECTORY

The Joomla Extension Directory (JED) is the official marketplace for Joomla extensions, including plugins. It's an excellent platform to promote and distribute your custom Joomla plugin to a larger audience of Joomla users. To distribute your plugin through the JED, you'll need to follow a few steps. Firstly, you'll have to prepare your plugin for submission, making sure to follow all the guidelines and requirements set forth by the JED team. This might include providing a detailed description and screenshot of your plugin, ensuring it works smoothly, and adhering to coding standards and security best practices. Once your plugin is ready, you can submit it to the JED for review. The review process can take several days to complete, during which time the JED team will test and evaluate your plugin to ensure it meets their standards and quality requirements. Assuming your plugin passes the review process, it will be published on the JED for users to download and use in their Joomla sites. You'll also have access to user ratings, feedback, and other relevant data that can help you improve your plugin over time. However, keep in mind that the JED is a competitive marketplace, and your plugin will be one of many available to users. To stand out, you'll need to develop a strong marketing strategy, including creating an engaging description, providing excellent customer support, and actively promoting your plugin through social media and other channels. Overall, the JED is an essential platform for any plugin developer looking to distribute their work to a larger audience of Joomla users. By following the guidelines, committing to high-quality code and security standards, and developing effective marketing strategies, you can succeed in the JED marketplace and find success in the Joomla community.

MARKETING AND PROMOTING YOUR PLUGIN

After creating your custom Joomla plugin, it's important to promote it to gain more exposure and downloads. Here are some strategies to market and promote your plugin:

1. Submitting Your Plugin to the Joomla Extension Directory

The first step to promoting your plugin is to submit it to the Joomla Extension Directory

(JED). The JED is the official directory for Joomla extensions, and it's where users go to find and install extensions. When submitting your plugin to the JED, make sure to provide a detailed description, screenshots, and a demo link to showcase its functionality. It's also important to keep your plugin updated and respond to user reviews and feedback.

2. Creating a Website and Social Media Pages for Your Plugin

Creating a website and social media pages for your plugin is crucial for its promotion. You can use your website as a platform to showcase your plugin's features, provide documentation and support, and announce updates and new releases. Similarly, social media pages such as Facebook and Twitter can help you reach a wider audience and engage with your users. Posting tutorials, videos, and testimonials can also help convince potential users to give your plugin a try.

3. Partnering with Other Developers and Websites

Partnering with other Joomla developers and websites can also help promote your plugin and increase its visibility. You can collaborate with other developers to create complementary plugins or submit guest posts on popular Joomla websites to showcase your plugin's features.

4. Offering Discounts and Incentives

Offering discounts and incentives is another effective way to promote your plugin and encourage users to download it. You can offer a limited-time discount on your plugin or provide bundled deals with other popular Joomla extensions.

5. Providing Excellent Support and Customer Service

Providing excellent support and customer service is crucial for keeping your users satisfied and promoting your plugin by word of mouth. Make sure to respond to user inquiries and issues promptly and provide comprehensive documentation to help your users get the most out of your plugin. In conclusion, promoting your Joomla plugin is just as important as creating it. By following these strategies, you can increase your plugin's visibility and reach a wider audience, leading to more downloads and satisfied users.

Chapter 6: Best Practices and Tips for Plugin Development

As a plugin developer, it's crucial to follow best practices and be aware of tips that can help you develop efficient and effective plugins. In this chapter, we'll cover some of the most important practices and tips that you should keep in mind while developing custom Joomla plugins.

SUBCHAPTER 6.1: CODE STANDARDS AND GUIDELINES

It's essential to follow code standards and guidelines while developing plugins. This will not only make your code more organized and readable, but it will also help you avoid errors and security vulnerabilities. Here are some best practices to follow:

1. Use Proper Indentation

Proper indentation helps you keep your code organized and readable. You should use spaces to indent your code and make sure that you use the correct number of spaces for each level of indentation.

2. Follow Naming Conventions

Following naming conventions makes your code easier to understand and maintain. You should give your plugins and plugin files descriptive names that reflect their purpose.

Additionally, you should follow standard naming conventions for variables, functions, classes, and methods.

3. Use Proper Commenting

Commenting your code is essential to help you and other developers understand what your code does. You should add comments to your code to explain complex logic or describe the purpose of functions and variables.

SUBCHAPTER 6.2: CHOOSING THE RIGHT PLUGIN TYPE

Joomla has different types of plugins that you can choose from depending on the functionality you want to add. Here are some common plugin types that you should be aware of:

1. Content Plugins

Content plugins allow you to add functionality to Joomla content. For example, you can create a content plugin that adds social media sharing buttons to your articles.

2. System Plugins

System plugins are used to modify Joomla's core functionality. These plugins are executed at different stages of Joomla's execution, and they can override core functions or add new ones.

3. User Plugins

User plugins are used to modify user-related functionality in Joomla. For example, you can create a user plugin that adds custom user profile fields.

SUBCHAPTER 6.3: TIPS FOR EFFICIENT PLUGIN DEVELOPMENT

Efficient plugin development is crucial if you want to create plugins that perform well and don't cause issues for your users. Here are some tips to keep in mind:

1. Avoid Duplicate Code

Avoiding duplicate code can save you a lot of time and effort in the long run. You should strive to create reusable code that you can use across different plugins or parts of your codebase.

2. Test Your Plugins

Testing your plugins is crucial to ensure that they work correctly and don't cause issues for your users. You should test your plugins thoroughly before releasing them to the public.

3. Keep Your Code Modular

Keeping your code modular makes it easier to maintain and modify in the future. You should strive to create small, reusable code modules that you can combine to create complex functionality. These are just a few tips and best practices that you should keep in mind while developing custom Joomla plugins. By following these practices and tips, you can create high-quality, efficient plugins that provide value to your users.

CODE STANDARDS AND GUIDELINES

When creating custom Joomla plugins, it is important to follow code standards and guidelines that have been established by the Joomla community. Consistent coding practices not only make your code easier to maintain, but also make it more accessible to other developers who may be working on your code in the future. One of the most important code standards to follow is to use proper naming conventions. This means that you should use descriptive names for functions, variables, and classes that accurately reflect their purpose and functionality. Another important guideline is to use proper code indentation to make your code more readable. Indentation makes it easier to distinguish between different code blocks and to see the structure and flow of your code. It is also important to properly document your code with comments. Comments should be used to explain the purpose of your code and how it relates to other parts of your plugin. This will make your code more understandable to others who may be reviewing or modifying it in the future. Finally, you should always sanitize and validate any user input that your plugin receives to prevent potential security vulnerabilities. This includes data from forms, URLs, and database queries. By following these established code standards and guidelines, you can create high-quality, reliable Joomla plugins that are both readable and maintainable.Choosing the right plugin type is crucial to the success of your Joomla website. There are a variety of plugin types to choose from, each with its own purpose and function. It's important to select the right plugin type for the specific job you want it to perform. Some plugins are designed for front-end functionality, such as enhancing the user experience, while others are geared towards back-end functionality, such as managing content or optimizing performance. It's essential to understand the various plugin types and their intended use cases. Here are some common plugin types to consider: 1. Content Plugins - These plugins are used to manipulate the content within Joomla. They can be used to add new tags, modify existing tags, or perform other tasks that affect the content's appearance. 2. System Plugins - These plugins operate at a lower level and can modify the Joomla core. This type of plugin can be used to implement security measures, or to alter the behavior of the front-end or back-end of the website. 3. Authentication Plugins - These plugins are used to control and regulate access to the front-end of your Joomla website. They can also be used to regulate access to different user groups or levels. 4. Search Plugins - These plugins are responsible for managing search functionality on your Joomla website. They can be used to customize search results, or to improve search speed and accuracy. 5. Language Plugins - These plugins enable the use of multiple languages on your Joomla website. They can be used to provide translations, or to customize the website's language settings. When choosing a plugin type, be sure to consider the specific needs of your website. By selecting the right plugin type, you can enhance your Joomla website's functionality and performance, and stay ahead of the competition.

SUBCHAPTER 6.3: TIPS FOR EFFICIENT PLUGIN DEVELOPMENT

Efficient plugin development is crucial to ensure that your project is completed in a timely and cost-effective manner. Here are some tips to help you with this process:

1. Plan Ahead

Before starting the development process, take some time to plan and structure your code. This can help you save time in the long run and prevent any potential errors.

2. Use Reusable Code

One of the best ways to increase efficiency is to use reusable code. This can save you a lot of time by not having to rewrite code from scratch for every plugin. You can use common functions and libraries that you have written or even incorporate open-source code.

3. Optimize Your Code

A key aspect of efficient plugin development is ensuring that your code runs smoothly and quickly. Although Joomla is built to handle plugins, poorly optimized code can slow down your website. Thus it is important to minimize HTTP requests and optimize your CSS and JavaScript.

4. Keep Up-to-Date with Joomla

Joomla is constantly evolving, so keeping up-to-date with the new features and updates can help you operate more efficiently. This will also improve your plugin development process and ensure your code is in line with the latest Joomla standards.

5. Use a Testing Methodology

Lastly, it is important to have a testing methodology in place. Proper testing can help you avoid any unforeseen issues with your code, and by catching bugs early on in the development process, you can save a lot of time and money. The standard Joomla testing methodology is with the use of Unit Testing which is a technique of testing individual pieces of source code to determine if they will work correctly when combined with other code, before relying on their function in a live environment. By following these tips, you can develop more efficient plugins and ensure that your project is completed within the given time-frame and budget.

Chapter 7: Troubleshooting and Common Errors

As a developer, you are bound to run into errors and issues while creating custom plugins for Joomla. This chapter will cover common errors that may occur during plugin development and how to troubleshoot them effectively.

SUBCHAPTER 7.1: DEBUGGING TIPS FOR PLUGIN DEVELOPERS

Debugging is a vital part of plugin development, as it helps identify errors and issues early on. Here are some tips to help you debug your custom Joomla plugins efficiently: **1. Use Debugging Tools:** Joomla offers a range of debugging tools such as error reporting, debug plugins, and tracing settings. These tools can help you identify and diagnose issues effectively. **2. Create Error Logs:** Creating error logs is an efficient way of tracking errors that occur during plugin development. You can use Joomla's logging APIs to create error logs and debug your code. **3. Test Your Plugins:** Always test your plugins after making changes or updates to your code. This will help you identify issues early on and fix them before releasing the plugin.

SUBCHAPTER 7.2: COMMON PLUGIN DEVELOPMENT ERRORS AND HOW TO FIX THEM

Here are some common errors that you may encounter during plugin development and how to fix them: **1. Plugin Not Working:** If your plugin is not working as expected, ensure that the plugin is enabled and that all the necessary files are present in the correct directories. You can also check Joomla's error log to identify and troubleshoot issues. **2. Plugin Conflicts:** Plugin conflicts may occur when two or more plugins are trying to accomplish the same task. To fix plugin conflicts, you can try disabling other plugins one by one until you identify the one causing the conflict. **3. Plugin Security Issues:** Ensuring the security of your custom Joomla plugin is crucial. Common security issues include SQL injection, cross-site scripting (XSS), and unauthorized access. To fix security issues, use Joomla's security APIs to validate user input and prevent common security attacks. By being aware of common errors and their solutions, you can save time and resources while developing custom plugins for Joomla. Remember to utilize debugging tools and test your plugins regularly to avoid issues and ensure smooth plugin functionality.Debugging your custom Joomla plugin is an important part of the development process. It allows you to find and fix errors and issues that may arise during plugin execution. In this section, we'll discuss some useful tips for debugging your custom Joomla plugin. One of the most effective ways to debug your Joomla plugin is by using print statements. Printing out variable values at different points in your code can help you identify where the issue is occurring. You can use the Joomla `JLog` class to output debug information to the Joomla log file. For example: ```php // Output debug information to Joomla log file JLog::add('My debug message', JLog::DEBUG); ``` Another helpful debugging tool is the Joomla Debug Console, which is available in Joomla 3.2 and later. The Debug Console provides a visual interface that allows you to track the execution of your code and view the contents of variables. You can enable the Debug Console by setting the `debug` configuration option to `true` in your `configuration.php` file, like this: ```php public $debug = true; ``` You can also use tools like Xdebug and PhpStorm to debug your Joomla plugin code. Xdebug is a PHP extension that provides advanced debugging features, such as profiling and code coverage analysis. PhpStorm is a popular PHP IDE that includes integrated debugging tools. When debugging your Joomla plugin, it's important to test your code in a variety of scenarios, such as different browsers, different user scenarios, and different Joomla configurations. This will help ensure that your plugin works correctly in all situations. In summary, debugging your Joomla plugin is an important step in the development process. By using print statements, the Joomla Debug Console, and other debugging tools, you can more effectively identify and fix issues in your code. Make sure to thoroughly test your plugin in different scenarios to ensure it works correctly for all users.

COMMON PLUGIN DEVELOPMENT ERRORS AND HOW TO FIX THEM

While plugin development can be an exciting and fulfilling experience, it is not uncommon to encounter errors. In fact, even seasoned developers will find themselves faced with bugs and other issues along the way. Fortunately, most common plugin development errors are easily recognizable and fixable. Here are some of the most common errors you may encounter, along with solutions on how to fix them:

1. Syntax Errors

Syntax errors can occur when there is a mistake in the plugin code that prevents it from executing properly. These errors are usually the result of a misplaced comma, semicolon, or bracket. To fix syntax errors, go through the plugin code line by line to check for any obvious mistakes. Be sure to pay attention to the error message that displays, as it will often give you a clue as to where the problem lies.

2. Undefined Variables

Undefined variable errors occur when a variable is referred to in the code but has not been defined in the plugin. This can be a simple typo or a misunderstanding of variable scope. To fix undefined variable errors, double-check your code to ensure that all variables have been properly defined and initialized before use. If you find any typos, correct them immediately.

3. Function Name Errors

Function name errors occur when you call a function that does not exist. This can happen when a function has been renamed or removed from the plugin code. To fix function name errors, check to make sure that all functions are properly defined and that the names match exactly where they are called. If needed, rename the function to match its new name.

4. White Screen of Death

The white screen of death is a common error that occurs when there is a fatal PHP error in the plugin code. This error results in a blank white screen instead of an error message. To fix the white screen of death error, first enable error reporting in your Joomla configuration. This will enable you to see the error message causing the issue. From there, you can troubleshoot and fix the problem.

5. Database Errors

Database errors can occur when there is an issue with database connectivity or SQL queries. These errors often present themselves as blank pages or error messages. To fix database errors, check to ensure that the database is properly configured and that all queries are properly written. If necessary, try running the queries directly in the database to identify issues. By being aware of these common plugin development errors and knowing how to fix them, you can avoid frustrating roadblocks in your development process. Remember to always double-check your code and make use of error messages to quickly and effectively troubleshoot any issues that arise.